Goodnight Teddy, Do Not Be Afraid

A Parable of Jesus

By Allison Wilhelmy

This Book Belongs to:

_____

Matthew 6:25-34

"That is why I tell you not to worry about everyday life—whether you have enough food and drink, or enough clothes to wear. Isn't life more than food, and your body more than clothing? Look at the birds. They don't plant or harvest or store food in barns, for your heavenly Father feeds them. And aren't you far more valuable to him than they are? Can all your worries add a single moment to your life?"

"And why worry about your clothing? Look at the lilies of the field and how they grow. They don't work or make their clothing, yet Solomon in all his glory was not dressed as beautifully as they are. And if God cares so wonderfully for wildflowers that are here today and thrown into the fire tomorrow, he will certainly care for you. Why do you have so little faith?"

"So don't worry about these things, saying, 'What will we eat? What will we drink? What will we wear?' These things dominate the thoughts of unbelievers, but your heavenly Father already knows all your needs. Seek the Kingdom of God above all else, and live righteously, and he will give you everything you need.

"So don't worry about tomorrow, for tomorrow will bring its own worries. Today's trouble is enough for today.

Baby Teddy tried to sleep.

But the room was cold,
and he had no socks on his feet.

Mama said, "Don't worry Teddy, do not be afraid. God gave you this blanket to hug you as you lay."

"He clothes flowers each year which come and go. How much more will He clothe your little toes?"

Matthew 6:28–29

But the room was dark and Teddy began to fear.

There was no more light because night was here.

Daddy said, "Do not worry Teddy, do not fear. God will bring light again and sun to warm your ears."

"He put the moon in the sky to help you sleep. Why then would you worry when God knows your needs?"

Matthew 6:31-32

But winter was coming and Teddy was hungry. When tomorrow comes will I have any honey?

Mama said, "Do not worry Teddy, do not be afraid. Life is more than the food we eat today."

"God cares how the birds get their food. And if He cares for them won't he care for you?"

Matthew 6: 25-27

Daddy said, "Goodnight Teddy, today will end soon. Seek God first and He will be with you."

Matthew 6:33

Mama said, "Goodnight Teddy, don't worry about tomorrow. Let tomorrow worry about itself and its own trouble."

Matthew 6:34

Teddy said, "Goodnight, sleep tight, I won't be afraid tonight! Because I know God cares for me and sees my needs."

The End

Romans 8:32; 35-37

Since He (God) did not spare even his own Son but gave him up for us all, won't he also give us everything else?... Can anything ever separate us from Christ's love? Does it mean he no longer loves us if we have trouble or calamity, or are persecuted, or hungry, or destitute, or in danger, or threatened with death? As the Scriptures say, "For your sake we are killed every day; we are being slaughtered like sheep." No, despite all these things, overwhelming victory is ours through Christ, who loved us.

Matthew 7: 7-11

"Keep on asking, and you will receive what you ask for. Keep on seeking, and you will find. Keep on knocking, and the door will be opened to you. For everyone who asks, receives. Everyone who seeks, finds. And to everyone who knocks, the door will be opened.

"You parents—if your children ask for a loaf of bread, do you give them a stone instead? Or if they ask for a fish, do you give them a snake? Of course not! So if you sinful people know how to give good gifts to your children, how much more will your heavenly Father give good gifts to those who ask him.

Goodnight Teddy, Do Not Be Afraid by Allison Wilhelmy
Published by Allison Wilhelmy

Copyright © 2025 Allison Wilhelmy
ISBN: 9798311370424

Made in the USA
Monee, IL
24 February 2025

12870796R10017